Easter

Program Builder No. 33

LILLENAS® DRAMA

Easter

Program Builder No. 33

Creative Resources for Program Directors

Compiled by
Kim Messer

lillenas
PUBLISHING COMPANY
Kansas City, MO 64141

Questions? Please write or call:
Lillenas Publishing Company
Drama Resources
P. O. Box 419527
Kansas City, MO 64141
Phone: 816-931-1900 • Fax: 816-412-8390
E-mail: drama@lillenas.com
Web Site: www.lillenasdrama.com

Executive Editor: Kim Messer

Copy Editor: Kimberly Meiste

Manuscript Formatting: Karen Phillips

Cover Design by Kevin Williamson

Contents

Recitations for Preschool

Our Father's Love

God, our Father's love
　　Is deep and true.
He cares about people
　　Like me and you.
He sent His Son, Jesus
　　To show us *the way*,
So we may live in heaven
　　With Him some day.

by Dorothy Heibel

Jesus, Jesus, Jesus

Jesus, Jesus, Jesus,
What a wonderful name we call.
Jesus, Jesus, Jesus,
For He rose to save us all.

by L. Ruth Carter

He Lives

Christ our Savior
Arose from the grave
And lives forever,
Our lives to save.

by Dorothy Heibel

Jesus

Jesus is *real*,
He can *heal*!

by Dorothy Heibel

Christ Is Risen

Child 1: Christ is risen; He is risen indeed.

Child 2: Life's victory is won.

Child 3: Christ is risen; He is risen indeed.

Child 4: A new day is begun.

Child 1: Christ is risen; He is risen indeed.

Child 2: Sing happy songs of praise.

Child 3: Christ is risen; He is risen indeed.

Child 4: Shout loud and glad hands raise.

by L. Ruth Carter

An Easter Message

(4 BUNNIES *each holding a large cardboard Easter Egg in bright colors. Costuming is optional.)*

BUNNY 1: I wish I were an Easter Bunny.

BUNNY 2: I'd hop and hop all day.

BUNNY 3: And as I hopped through the Easter grass . . .

BUNNY 4: This is what I'd say:

(They turn their eggs over and read the word printed on the back of each egg.)

BUNNY 1: Jesus

BUNNY 2: Christ

BUNNY 3: Lives

BUNNY 4: Today!

(End there
or
repeat the last four lines for fun.)

by Dorothy Heibel

Recitations for Ages 5 to 7

An Easter Welcome

Welcome on this Easter day.
We're all so glad you came.
Listen closely to our words
(put hand up to ears)
So you will not go home the same.

by Iris Gray Dowling

Eternal Salvation

To the great God
Of all creation,
Thank You for Christ,
Our eternal salvation.

by Robert Colbert

Joyous News

Have you seen Christ Jesus?
He is risen; He's alive!
That joyful news we shout and sing . . .
O'er all the earth He reigns as King!

by Dorothy Heibel

Praise the Lord!

(Use one or more expressive children for this recitation.)

Praise the Lord!
Jesus is *risen*!
Praise the Lord!

He came to save us
From our sin.
Praise the Lord!

His love will
Never, ever end.
Praise the Lord!

He was buried
And rose again.
Praise the Lord!

Praise the Lord!
Jesus is *risen*!
Praise the Lord!

by Susan Harrison

Jesus Is Lord!

It's time to dance,
It's time to sing,
Jesus is Lord
Of everything!

by Dorothy Heibel

Spring

Do you know
Who melts the snow
And makes the flowers
Begin to grow?
Who brings the leaves
Back to the trees,
And makes the warm
In the breeze?
It's God, our Father
Who brings the spring,
And with it *new life*
To everything.

by Dorothy Heibel

The Story

You all know the story,
And yes, it is true.
Christ rose from the dead
To save me and you.

If you want to believe
It's all your choice.
He really loves you
And wants you to rejoice.

by Susan Harrison

God's Promise

What a wonderful promise:
Jesus lives!
And to each one of us
New life He gives!

by Dorothy Heibel

Some Say

(Have one child read expressively,
or give verses to two or more children
to say from memory.)

Some say He was nice,
    Some say He had appeal,
Some say He was a prophet,
    Some say the real deal.

What matters is what you think.
    What is it that you say?
How do you define Him?
    Is He the only way?

I know Him personally.
    There's no doubt at all
He is the real Savior
    Who catches me when I fall.

He died and rose again.
    He did it all for love.
There is no other way
    To get to heaven above.

by Susan Harrison

Recitations for Ages 8 to 10

Joy Came in the Morning

Mary's life had lost all its hope.
For awhile she forgot what Jesus had said.
She knew her friend had died on a cross,
Then her joy returned when He rose from the dead.

by Iris Gray Dowling

Love Was Shown

Love was shown upon the/that cross.
Jesus paid the ultimate/priceless cost.
He cried "forgive them" to the sky.
He gave His life in exchange for mine.

by Kimberly Meiste

Peter's Love

Peter wanted to follow the Lord.
At times he boldly stepped ahead.
Then sadly he denied his Lord three times,
(Hold up three fingers)
But forgiven he showed his love instead.
(Arms over chest; love sign)

by Iris Gray Dowling

Adult Readings & Recitations

At Easter

Daffodils are blooming
    With the color of the sun.
Birds are celebrating spring
    With hopping, chirping fun.
Easter comes with springtime
    And all its warmth and love.
When earth awakens from winter's sleep,
    We thank the Lord above!

by Dorothy Heibel

Easter Is Here!

Crocuses beneath the snow
Promise an end to winter's woe.
Easter comes and ends earth's sadness.
Christ's resurrection brings us gladness!

by Dorothy Heibel

The Rest of the Prophesy

by George Halitzka

Running Time: 2-3 minutes

Theme: Living for or hiding from Christ

Suggested Use: Good Friday

Scripture References: Isaiah 53; Luke 23:50-24:14

Production Notes: Follow this story with the Afro-American Spiritual, *Were You There?*, ideally sung a cappella by a soloist. Gripping art images of the tomb and the various visitors to it can be shown onscreen during the reading. The final image is an angel standing inside the empty tomb.

STORYTELLER: Nobody really expected the rest of the prophesy to come true.

The first part of Isaiah's prediction had already been fulfilled—the "despised and rejected," "smitten and afflicted" part. But the rest of the story—where it said Jesus would "see His offspring" and "prolong His days"—nobody really believed *that* part. The disciples were all playing ostrich in some rented room on the wrong side of the tracks. Jesus' mother and Mary Magdalene went to the tomb. However, they only went to find out where they should come to embalm Him later. The Jewish leaders didn't expect a resurrection; their only interest was preventing a hoax.

Now Jesus' death did bring a couple of "closet disciples" into the open, but even they weren't looking for miracles. Joseph of Arimathea was a secret member of Christ's fan club who also served on the Jewish ruling council. He found the guts to ask Pilate for Jesus' body. Nicodemus, who wouldn't be caught dead with Jesus before, came along to help. Maybe those two figured if Jesus was gone, they couldn't get in trouble anymore. Maybe they felt guilty for not sticking by Him when He was alive, and decided to do too little, too late. But in any case, they definitely expected the Rabbi to stay dead!

And very little has changed in two thousand years. Jesus still has "closet disciples" like Joseph, who won't admit to knowing Him until it's perfectly safe. Others, like Peter and the boys, run away at the first sign of danger. Some claim to follow Him, but, like the Mary's, only visit the cross and the tomb—they don't encounter the risen Christ. Some Pharisees still care more about maintaining the *status quo* than encountering the Messiah.

But at least all of them had an excuse—the resurrection hadn't happened yet. They had every reason to expect Jesus to stay in the tomb; every reason to believe their Messiah-radar had malfunctioned; every reason to think Jesus wasn't actually God. You don't.

This Easter, are you living radically in the light of the resurrection? Or like Joseph and Nicodemus, would you prefer to hide until it's too late—and live like Jesus stayed dead?

Veil of Darkness

by George Halitzka

Running Time: 1-2 minutes

Theme: God and man reconciled

Scripture Reference: Matthew 27:45-56

Suggested Use: Good Friday

Cast:

STORYTELLER 1

STORYTELLER 2

Production Notes: The Storytellers begin in a single spotlight. Where the text indicates a brief "pause," the light is extinguished, leaving the narrators in darkness except for two candles. At the end of the reading, they can blow out both candles. This reading should be followed with a brief silence.

STORYTELLER 1: It was thick and complete—not a storm; not an eclipse.

STORYTELLER 2: A veil of shadows thicker and more fearsome than night enveloped Skull Hill. Wrath shattered rocks; justice shook the firmament.

STORYTELLER 1: From every soul in every village in every nation, treachery, and greed, and debauchery, and idolatry, and deceit had been collected, drawn with irresistible force, and concentrated with crushing intensity on the dislocated shoulders of a broken human body.

STORYTELLER 2: Now a veil of blackness broke the communion of the Father and the Son, intact since eternity—a separation of holiness from the sin of the world.

STORYTELLER 1: The intimate fellowship of God and God that will never end; a marriage of Essences inconceivable to limited, flesh-bound humans—was broken.

STORYTELLER 2: Purity himself could not gaze upon filth. The veil of darkness fell between Father and Son.

(Pause)

STORYTELLER 1: It is customary at Easter to discuss the process of crucifixion in great detail.

STORYTELLER 2: The thorns; the nails; the blood; the spear.

STORYTELLER 1: But the greatest suffering Jesus endured was none of the above.

STORYTELLER 2: When the Son of Man was crushed by every sin and the eternal intimacy of the Trinity was torn asunder—that was the moment when Jesus' soul screamed in agony. He cried out when the veil of darkness fell.

STORYTELLER 1: "My God, my God, why have You forsaken me?"

STORYTELLER 2: Never were truer words spoken.

STORYTELLER 1: Jesus, who had known nothing but love for all eternity . . . was abandoned by its Source when darkness fell.

Scripts and Plays

Only Believe

by Iris Gray Dowling

Running Time: 15 minutes with music

Synopsis: A readers theatre using biblical characters. Readers tell the resurrection story paraphrased from the four Gospels

Cast:

NARRATOR

SOLDIER

MARY

ANGELS

PETER

JOHN

JESUS

THOMAS

Props:

Three pictures for projecting at the designated times:

1) The empty cross
2) The empty tomb
3) The risen Christ with nail prints in hands

Sound Effects: An earthquake thundering sound made by hand hitting on the low notes of a piano.

(Readers stand or sit onstage dressed in black. Lights are dimmed except at the end.)

Opening Instrumental Music: *The Old Rugged Cross* (Picture of empty cross)

NARRATOR: Jesus died on a Roman cross and was buried in a rich man's tomb. The soldiers sealed the tomb with a large stone over the doorway.

SOLDIER: Jesus will not get out of that tomb. His friends are not going to steal His body and say He arose from the dead. We will guard this tomb day and night!

Musical Solo: *Christ Arose* (Using verses 1 and 2, no chorus)

SFX: Earthquake (Hit low piano keys with a full hand)

NARRATOR: Very early Sunday morning an angel rolled the stone away and sat on it. The soldiers fell into a daze. Jesus arose from the grave.

(Project the empty tomb picture to remain on the screen until the end)

Musical Solo: *Christ Arose* (Verse 3 and chorus)

NARRATOR: Mary and the women brought sweet-smelling spices to anoint Jesus' body, hoping they could get near the tomb. They were amazed to see the soldiers dazed.

MARY: Look! The stone that blocked the door is moved. Who's that sitting there? The tomb seems light inside. We were a little frightened and almost turned around to leave when the man in white spoke.

ANGEL: Don't be afraid. You are looking for Jesus, the Nazarene, who was crucified. He is not dead! He is risen! He is not here! Look! See the place where they laid Him. Go tell the disciples and Peter about this. You'll see Jesus in Galilee. Remember what He told you?

MARY: Let's go find Peter and John.

Musical Solo: *Christ the Lord Is Risen Today* (Verses 2 and 3)

MARY: Peter, someone took Jesus out of the tomb and we don't know where He is!

PETER: John, let's go see.

Transition Music: *Hallelujah! What a Savior!*

JOHN: His burial clothes are folded here. Where could He be?

PETER: There's the cloth that was around His head. He must *not* be dead, but where is He?

MARY: Did they take Him away?

JOHN: He is not here. Let's go look for Him. But where shall we look?

PETER: Come on, John. Let's go home toward Galilee.

Musical Solo: *The Way of the Cross Leads Home* (Verse 1)

MARY: I can't leave here. *(Cries)* Look! There are two angels in the tomb now. One is at the place of His head and the other where His feet were laid.

ANGEL: Woman, why are you crying?

MARY *(sobbing):* They took away my Lord and I don't know where they have laid Him.

ANGEL: Mary, He is alive. He is risen from the dead. He will see you soon.

JESUS: Mary, why do you weep? Who do you seek?

MARY: I thought He was the gardener so I turned around and said, "Sir, if you know where He is, please tell me?"

JESUS: Mary.

MARY: Master! *(Speaks as if recognizing him)*

JESUS: Mary, don't touch Me yet. I have to ascend to My heavenly Father. Go, tell My followers that I am alive.

Musical Solo: *Oh, It Is Wonderful* (Verses 1 and 2)

(Picture of the risen Christ with nail-scarred hands)

NARRATOR: Mary told the disciples she had seen Jesus and that He spoke to her. Later that day the disciples were gathered in a room, except for Thomas. The door was locked for fear of the authorities. Jesus appeared in their midst.

JESUS: Peace be with you. Why are there doubts in your minds? Look and you will see the nail prints in My hands and the wound in My side. Touch Me and believe.

DISCIPLES: It is really You, Lord!

JESUS: You must go tell the good news to everyone you see.

Musical Solo: *Wounded for Me* (Verses 3, 4, and 5)

NARRATOR: Jesus left the room the same way He came in. The other disciples told Thomas Jesus had appeared to them. He did not believe it.

THOMAS: Except I see and put my finger in the nail prints of His hands and put my hand in His side, I will not believe.

Musical Solo: *Almost Persuaded* (Verse 1)

NARRATOR: Eight days later he got the chance to do that. Jesus appeared to the disciples again. Thomas was with them this time. Jesus spoke directly to Thomas.

JESUS: Thomas, put your finger in these prints of the nails in My hands and put your hand in My wounded side. Don't stay faithless, but do believe.

THOMAS: My Lord and my God, I believe! *(Says meekly and sincerely)*

JESUS: Thomas, because you saw Me, you believed; blessed are they who have not felt or seen My scarred hands, but believe.

NARRATOR: "Jesus did many other miraculous signs in the presence of His disciples which are not recorded in this book. But these are written that you may believe that Jesus is the Christ, the Son of God and that be believing, you may have life in His name." John 20:31

Musical Solo: *Because He Lives* (Verses 1 and 3)

NARRATOR: Jesus said He must die and rise again so we could have forgiveness of sins. Today, there are still those who doubt and those who believe. Which one are you?

Closing Song: *Only Believe* (Audience sings verses 1 and 3)

O, Glorious Day!

by L. Ruth Carter

Running Time: Approximately 15 minutes

Theme: An answer to those critics who denied the divine nature of Jesus Christ

Scripture References: Psalm 32:2; Isaiah 53; Luke 23; John 1:1-4, 1:10, 12, 19; Romans 3:31, 4:24, 8:1-3, 31-39; James 5:8; Philippians 2:7; 1 Thessalonians 2:19, 3:12-13; 1 John 3:1, 4:9-10

Synopsis: A worship service built around the great gospel hymn, *One Day*, by J. Wilbur Chapman, Pastor / Evangelist / Revivalist of the late 19th and early 20th centuries.

Cast:

NARRATOR 1

NARRATOR 2

READER

Production Notes: Based on the gospel hymn, *One Day*, each of the five verses focuses on a different element of Jesus' life and ministry on earth and partners it to a line in the chorus that highlights an important doctrine of His work of salvation. The presentation of the hymn itself can be treated in many ways—congregational, choral, solo, etc. A different hymn tune may be used. While written for two narrators, one or more of the narrations can be adapted as responsive readings. Optional music is suggested.

Optional Choral Prelude

Optional Congregational Praise and Worship

Welcome by the Pastor

NARRATOR 1: In the beginning—God . . .

NARRATOR 2: It all began with God, didn't it? God, the Alpha and the Omega, the beginning and the end.

NARRATOR 1: And in the beginning was the Word. The Word. The Word was with God and the Word was God.

NARRATOR 2: Yes, it all began with God.

NARRATOR 1: In the beginning, God created the heaven and the earth. Through Him—through the Word—all things were made. Nothing was made without Him.

NARRATOR 2: And in God was life, in God was light. The life in God gave us light.

NARRATOR 1: But somehow, we who were in darkness could not understand the light, could not grab hold of the light—that light that was life in God. So God—the Word—came. He came to us. He came into the world. He, God, the Creator of the Universe, stepped into time, took the nature of a servant and became a human.

NARRATOR 2: He dwelt among us. Living, He loved us. Living, He loved *me*!

Song (Verse 1): *One Day*, by J. Wilbur Chapman

One day when heaven was filled with His praises,
One day when sin was as black as can be,
Jesus came forth to be born of a virgin,
Dwelt among men—my Example is He!

Chorus: Living, He loved me;
Dying, He saved me;
Buried, He carried my sins far away;
Rising, He justified freely forever;
One day He's coming—O glorious day!

NARRATOR 2: Living, He loved us.

NARRATOR 1: By dwelling among us, the infinite God subjected himself to the limitations of time and space so that all who believe in His name would have the right to become His children.

NARRATOR 2: Wow! Just think how much the Father loves us. Think about it. He loves us so much that He lets us be called His children. His children!

NARRATOR 1: And we truly are His children.

NARRATOR 2: OK, so we know God loves us. But do you know how He showed it? He showed His love for us—yes, for you and me—when He sent His Son, His only Son, into the world to give us life.

Optional Testimony

Optional Music (suggestions): *Beauty of the Lord; If That Isn't Love; Jesus, Lover of My Soul; Jesus Loves Me; Light of the World; Love Was When; Such Love*

NARRATOR 1: Now here's something really exciting. It's about true love. We all want true love, don't we? Well, true love isn't our love for God. Yup, you heard me. It's not our love for Him, but it's His love for us. Yeah, I'm going to say that again. True love is God's love for us.

NARRATOR 2: So, God sent His Son into the world to give us life.

NARRATOR 1: Living, He loved us.

NARRATOR 2: God sent His Son to be the sacrifice by which our sins are forgiven.

NARRATOR 1: Dying, He saved us. Dying, He saved *me*!

Song (Verse 2): *One Day*

One day they led Him up Calvary's mountain;
One day they nailed Him to die on the tree.
Suffering anguish, despised and rejected,
Bearing our sins—my Redeemer is He!

Chorus: Living, He loved me;
Dying, He saved me;
Buried, He carried my sins far away;
Rising, He justified freely forever;
One day He's coming—O glorious day!

NARRATOR 1: Dying, He saved us.

NARRATOR 2: And on that day, He was led up the mountain to the Place of the Skull. There He was nailed to the cross.

NARRATOR 1: He was a man of sorrows. He knew suffering and grief.

NARRATOR 2: The leaders insulted Him. "Ha, ha, He says He is the Savior," they jeered. "He came to save others, now let Him save himself."

NARRATOR 1: He was despised. He was rejected.

NARRATOR 2: The soldiers laughed. "If you are the King of the Jews, save yourself."

NARRATOR 1: He was oppressed. He was afflicted.

NARRATOR 2: Two thieves were crucified with Him. One of the thieves mocked Him, "Aren't you the Savior?" he cried. "Save yourself and save us too." He was despised. He was rejected.

NARRATOR 1: But the other thief said, "Don't you fear God? Can't you see that He is getting the same punishment as us? And that He did nothing to deserve it? We got what was coming to us, but this Man is innocent."

NARRATOR 2: He was wounded for our transgressions. He was bruised for our iniquities.

NARRATOR 1: And the thief turned to Jesus and said, "Remember me." And Jesus promised him, "Today you will be with Me in paradise."

NARRATOR 2: And by His stripes we are healed."

NARRATOR 1: When Jesus knew that the time had come, He said, "I am thirsty." They soaked a sponge in sour wine and held it to His lips at the end of a hyssop branch. When He had tasted it, He said, "It is finished." Salvation was won.

NARRATOR 2: He suffered the punishment that freed us and gave us peace. He bore the iniquity of us all. Dying He saved us.

Optional Music (suggestions): *And Can It Be?; At the Foot of the Cross; Beautiful, Scandalous Night; Behold the Lamb; Blessed Redeemer; Feel the Nails; He Was Wounded for Our Transgressions; I Will Sing the Wondrous Story; Lamb of God; Meekness and Majesty; My Tribute; One Drop of Blood; The Calvary Road; There Stood a Lamb; Via Dolorosa; Watch the Lamb*

Optional Testimony

NARRATOR 1: The Lord is my rock, my fortress, my Savior.

NARRATOR 2: Dying, He saved us.

NARRATOR 1: Buried, He carried our sins far away. Buried, He carried *my* sins far away!

Song (Verse 3): *One Day*

One day they left Him alone in the garden;
Onc day He rested, from suffering free.
Angels came down o'er His tomb to keep vigil.
Hope of the hopeless—my Savior is He!

Chorus: Living, He loved me;
Dying, He saved me;
Buried, He carried my sins far away;
Rising, He justified freely forever;
One day He's coming—O glorious day!

NARRATOR 1: Buried, He carried our sins far away.

NARRATOR 2: When we belong to Jesus, we don't get the punishment we deserve. Life in Jesus Christ frees us from sin and death. God set us free when He sent His Son to be just like us sinners. He sent Him to be a sacrifice for our sin.

Optional Music (suggested): *Above All*; *Jesus Paid It All*; *Lamb of God* [*Agnus Dei*]. Songs from the second group would work here as well.

NARRATOR 1: Is anything better than this? God is on our side! How can anyone be against us?

NARRATOR 2: If God accepts us, how can anyone else condemn us?

NARRATOR 1: Can anything separate us from the love of Jesus?

NARRATOR 2: No!

NARRATOR 1: Can angels or demons?

NARRATOR 2: No!

NARRATOR 1: Can the present or the future?

NARRATOR 2: No!

NARRATOR 1: Can the powers above or the powers below?

NARRATOR 2: No! Nothing can separate us from God's love, which is in Jesus Christ our Lord!

Optional Testimony

NARRATOR 2: Buried, He carried our sins far away.

NARRATOR 1: Rising, He justified, freely forever. Rising, He justified freely forever!

Song (Verse 4): *One Day*

One day the grave could conceal Him no longer;
One day the stone rolled away from the door.
Then He arose—over death He had conquered;
Now is ascended, my Lord evermore!

Chorus: Living, He loved me;
Dying, He saved me;
Buried, He carried my sins far away;
Rising, He justified freely forever;
One day He's coming—O glorious day!

NARRATOR 1: Rising, He justified, freely forever.

NARRATOR 2: Rejoice!

NARRATOR 1: He was handed over to death because of our sins.

NARRATOR 2: Rejoice!

NARRATOR 1: God holds no record of our sins.

NARRATOR 2: Rejoice!

NARRATOR 1: When we trust Jesus to take away our sin, we are made right in God's sight.

NARRATOR 2: Rejoice!

NARRATOR 1: He has declared us not guilty.

NARRATOR 2: Rejoice!

NARRATOR 1: Rising, He justified, freely forever.

Optional Music (suggestions): *Celebrate Jesus; Christ the Lord Is Risen Today; Crown Him with Many Crowns; He That Is in Us; I Believe in Jesus; I Know that My Redeemer Lives; I've Just Seen Jesus; Rise Again; The Easter Song; Thine Is the Glory*

READER: Luke 24:1-12

Optional Testimony (could be meditation from pastor)

NARRATOR 1: Rising, He justified, freely forever. One day He's coming, O, glorious day! One day He's coming—O, glorious day!

Song (Verse 5): *One Day*

One day the trumpet will sound for His coming;
One day the skies with His glories will shine.
Wonderful day, my beloved ones bringing!
Glorious Savior—this Jesus is mine!

Chorus: Living, He loved me;
Dying, He saved me;
Buried, He carried my sins far away;
Rising, He justified freely forever;
One day He's coming—O glorious day!

NARRATOR 2: One day He's coming—O glorious day!

NARRATOR 1: One day the trumpet will sound for His coming.

NARRATOR 2: O what joy! O what hope! We stand together before our Lord Jesus when He returns.

NARRATOR 1: One day the skies with His glory will shine.

NARRATOR 2: May the Lord make our love for each other grow and expand. May our love for everyone overflow. When Jesus comes with all who belong to Him, He will make us strong, clean, and holy to stand before God.

NARRATOR 1: Wonderful day, my beloved ones bringing.

NARRATOR 2: Wait patiently for the coming of the Lord. Take courage, for that day, that glorious day is near.

NARRATOR 1: Glorious Savior, this Jesus is mine!

NARRATOR 2: One day He's coming—O, glorious day!

Optional Music (suggestions): *All Hail King Jesus; I Can Only Imagine; Is It the Crowning Day?; Jesus, We Just Want to Thank You; Lift Up Your Heads; Majesty; Some Golden Daybreak; The King Is Coming; The Lion and the Lamb; These Are the Days of Elijah; This Could Be the Dawning of That Day; We Shall Behold Him; Worthy Is the Lamb*

Final Music: Sing the chorus of *One Day*